MW01290869

FLASHCARD BOOKS

HOUSEHOLD ITEMS

ENGLISH
to
GERMAN

FLASHCARD BOOK

BLACK & WHITE EDITION

HOW TO USE:

- READ THE ENGLISH WORD ON THE FIRST PAGE.

- IF YOU KNOW THE TRANSLATION SAY IT OUT LOUD.

- TURN THE PAGE AND SEE IF YOU GOT IT RIGHT.

- IF YOU GUESSED CORRECTLY, WELL DONE!
IF NOT, TRY READING THE WORD USING THE PHONETIC PRONUNCIATION GUIDE.

- NOW TRY THE NEXT PAGE.
THE MORE YOU PRACTICE THE BETTER YOU WILL GET!

BOOKS IN THIS SERIES:
ANIMALS
NUMBERS SHAPES AND COLORS
HOUSEHOLD ITEMS
CLOTHES

ALSO AVAILABLE IN OTHER LANGUAGES INCLUDING:

FRENCH, GERMAN, SPANISH, ITALIAN,

RUSSIAN, CHINESE, JAPANESE AND MORE.

WWW.FLASHCARDEBOOKS.COM

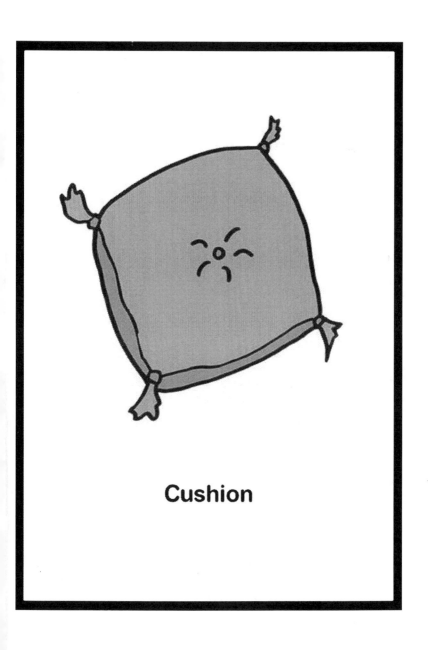

Cushion

Das Kissen

kiss-en

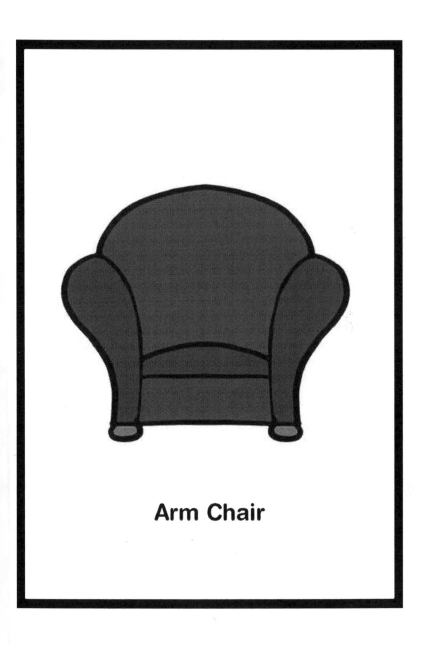

Arm Chair

Der Sessel

seh-sell

Sofa

Das Sofa

So-fa

Chair

Der Stuhl

Sh-tool

Fireplace

Der Kamin

Kah-meen

Magazine

Das Magazin

ma-ga-zeen

PC

Der PC

pe-tseh

Television

Der Fernseher

fern-seh-her

Remote Control

Die Fernbedienung

fern-beh-dee-noong

Speakers

Die Lautsprecher

loud-sprech-her

Laptop

Der Laptop

laptop

Fish Tank

Das Aquarium

a-kwa-rioom

Light Bulb

Die Glühbirne

glueeh-birneh

Rug

Der Teppich

tepp-ich

Clock

Die Uhr

oor

Keys

Die Schlüssel

schlueh-sell

Iron

Das Bügeleisen

buu-gell-i-zen

Plant

Die Pflanze

pflahn-tze

Table

Der Tisch

Tisch

Photo Frame

Der Bilderrahmen

bill-der-rah-men

Light Switch

Der Lichtschalter

licht-schall-terr

Balloon

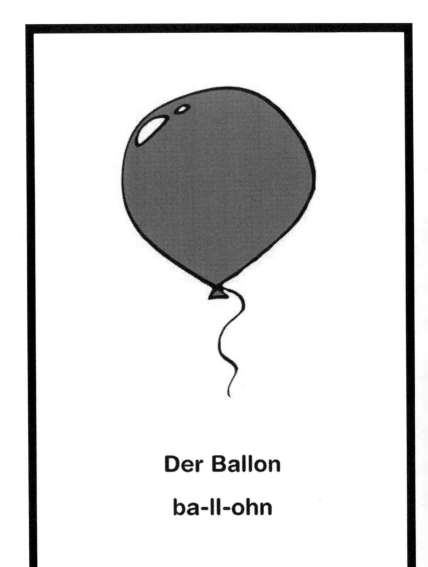

Der Ballon

ba-ll-ohn

Bed

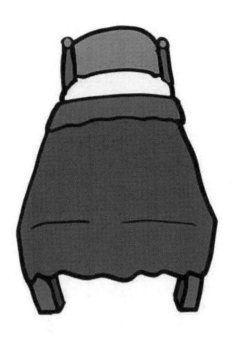

Das Bett

bet

Double Bed

Das Doppelbett

dop-pell-bet

Bunk Bed

Das Etagenbett

eh-tah-gen-bet

Lamp

Die Lampe

lahm-pe

Pillow

Das Kissen

kiss-sen

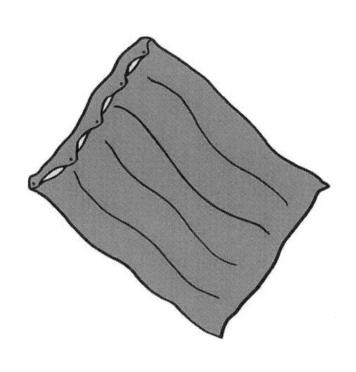

Duvet

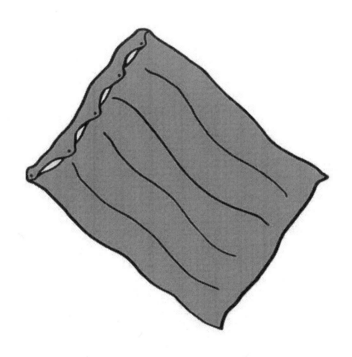

Die Daunendecke

downen-deh-keh

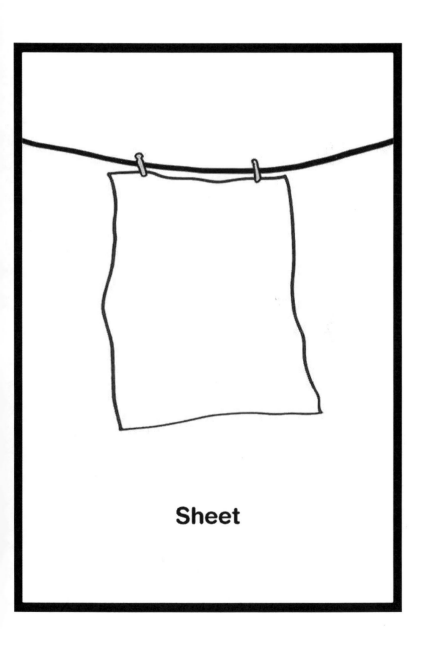

Sheet

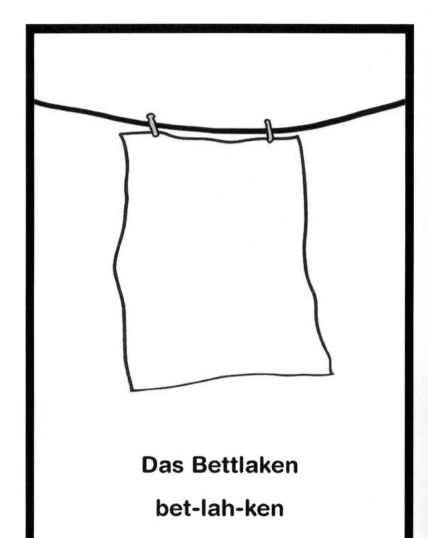

Das Bettlaken

bet-lah-ken

Alarm Clock

Der Wecker

weh-kerr

Crib

Das Kinderbett

Kin-derr-bet

Wardrobe

Der Kleiderschrank

clyde-er-shrunk

Drawers

Die Kommode

komm-moh-deh

Cell Phone/Mobile

Das Handy

Handy

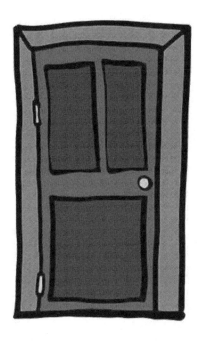

Door

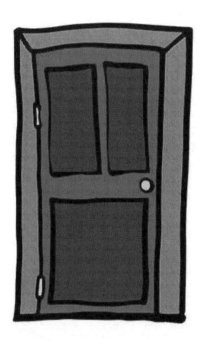

Die Türe

tue-reh

Window

Das Fenster

fan-ster

Roof

Das Dach

dach

Door Bell

Die Klingel

Kling-ell

Newspaper

Die Zeitung

zei-tung

Oven

Der Ofen

oh-fan

Microwave

Die Mikrowelle

mee-kro-well-eh

Toaster

Der Toaster

toaster

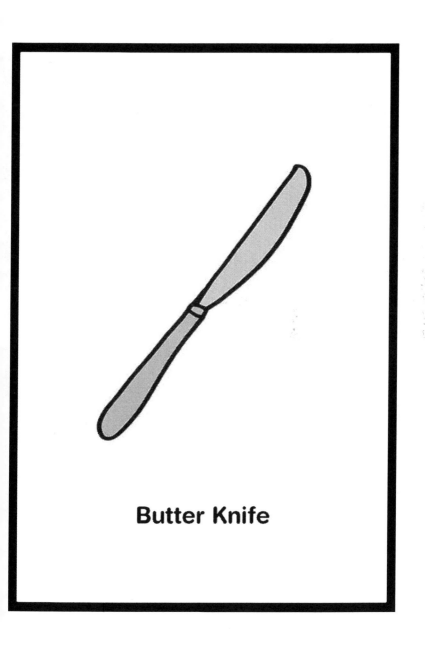

Butter Knife

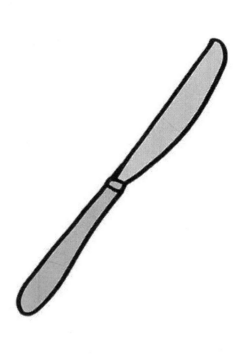

Das Buttermesser

boo-ter-mess-er

Fork

Die Gabel

gah-bell

Spoon

Der Löffel

leu-fell

Kitchen Sink

Das Spülbecken

spuel-back-en

Cupboard

Der Schrank

shrunk

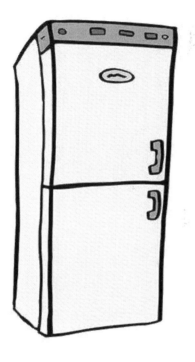

Fridge

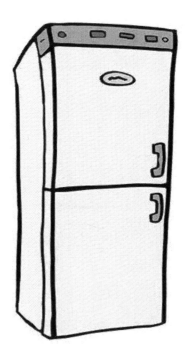

Der Kühlschrank

kuel-shrunk

Kettle

Der Kessel

kes-sell

Pans

Die Töpfe

Tup-fuh

Frying Pan

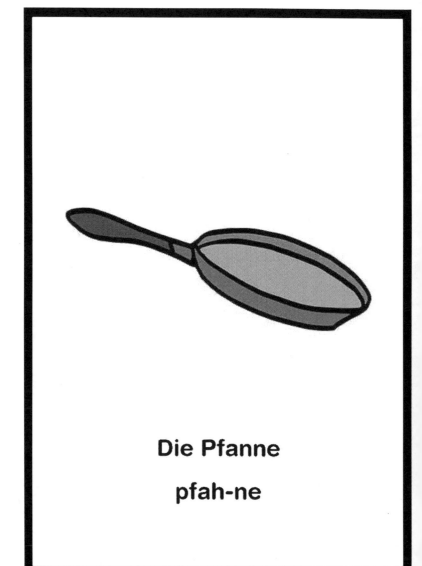

Die Pfanne

pfah-ne

Knife

Das Messer

mess-sir

Dishwasher

Die Spühlmaschine

spuehl-mah-schee-neh

Washing up Liquid

Das Spühlmittel

spuehl-mitt-el

Washing Machine

Die Waschmaschine

wash-mah-sheen-eh

Oil

Das Öl

euhl

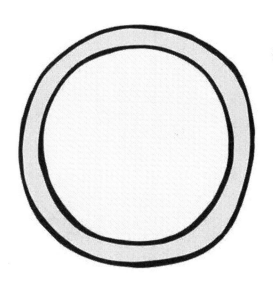

Plate

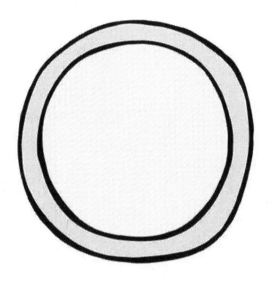

Der Teller

tell-ehrr

Cup

Die Tasse

tah-seh

Broom

Der Besen

beh-zen

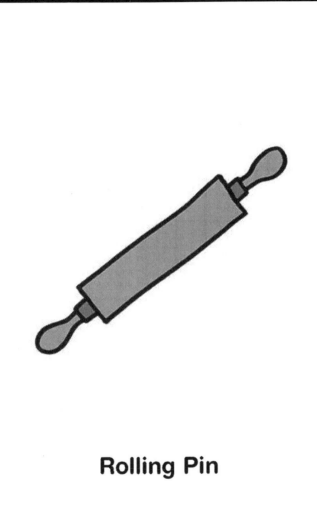

Rolling Pin

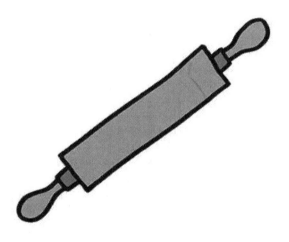

Das Nudelholz

noodle-holts

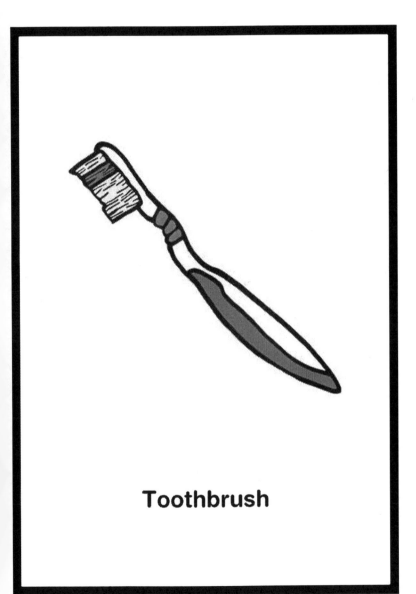

Toothbrush

Die Zahnbürste

tsan-bue-rste

Toothpaste

Die Zahnpasta

tsan-pass-tah

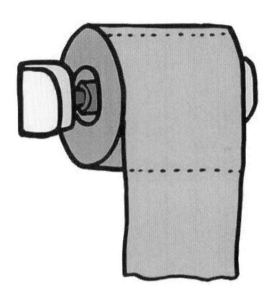

Toilet Paper

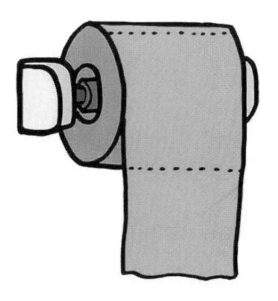

Das Klopapier

Klo-pah-peer

Shower

Die Dusche

doo-sheh

Soap

Die Seife

sai-feh

Tap

Der Wasserhahn

was-her-hahn

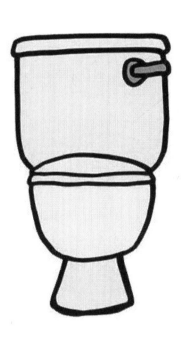

Toilet

Die Toilette

toilet-eh

Sink

Das Waschbecken

wash-back-ken

Bath

Das

bu-h-d

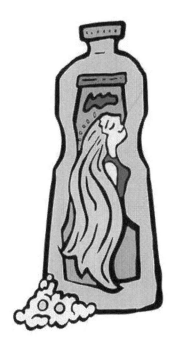

Shampoo

Das Shampoo

shawm-poh

Sponge

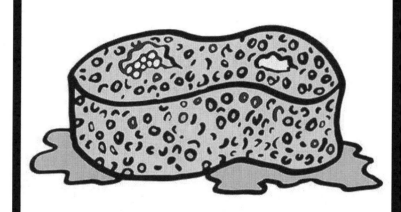

Der Schwamm

sh-wamm

Hairdryer

Der Föhn

foe-hn

Pencil Sharpener

Der Anspitzer

un-sh-pits-er

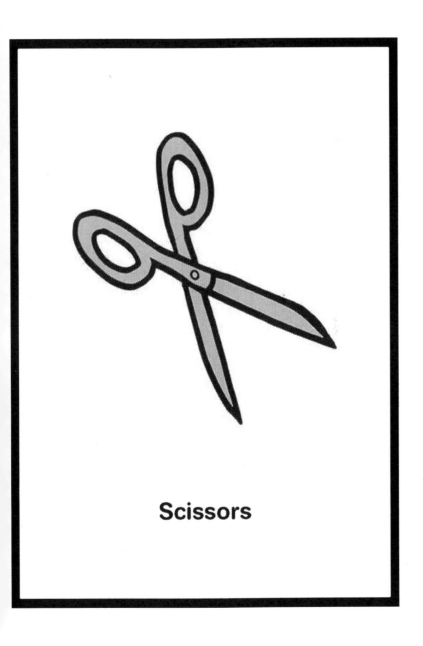

Scissors

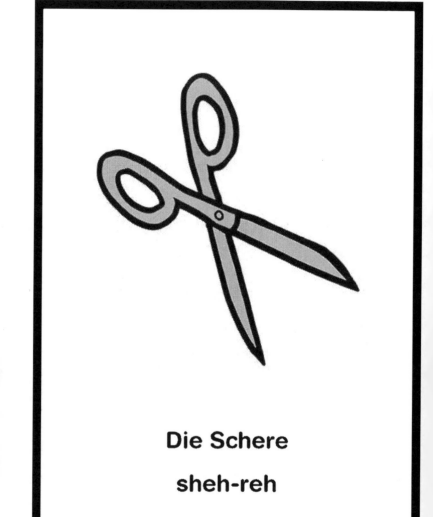

Die Schere

sheh-reh

Book Case

Der Bücherschrank

buu-cher-schrank

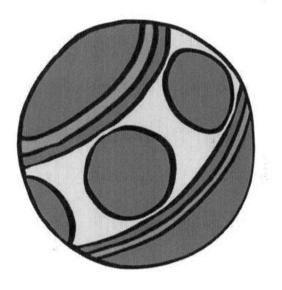

Ball

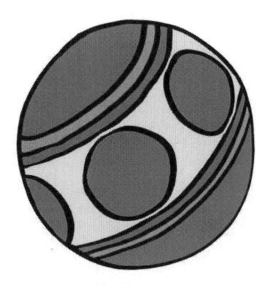

Der Ball

bah-ll

Doll

Die Puppe

puh-peh

Teddy Bear

Der Teddybär

teddy-bear

Castle

Das Schloss

sh-loss

Sandwich

Das Sandwich

sandwich

Corn Flakes

Die Cornflakes

cornflakes

Milk

Die Milch

mill-ch

Apple

Der Apfel

up-fell

Hammer

Der Hammer

Hum-err

Screwdriver

Der Schraubendreher

shrau-ben-dre-her

Screw

Die Schraube

shrau-beh

Nails

Die Nägel

neh-gel

Wrench/Spanner

Der Schraubenschlüssel

shrau-ben-shlue-sel

Shovel

Die Schaufel

shau-fell

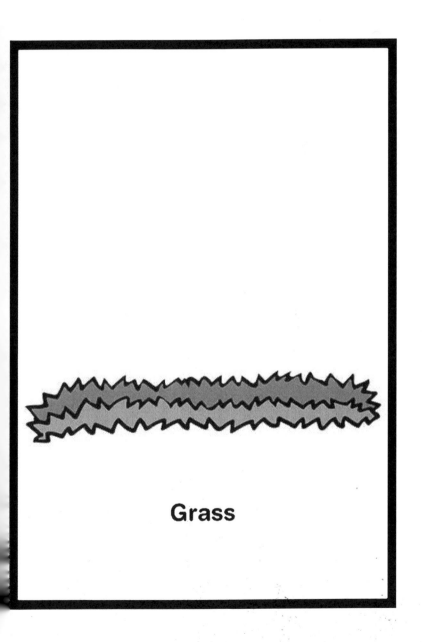

Grass

Das Gras

graas

Tree

Der Baum

baum

Green House

Das Gewächshaus

ge-wex-house

Lawn Mower

Der Rasenmäher

rah-zen-meh-her

Hose

Der Schlauch

sh-louch

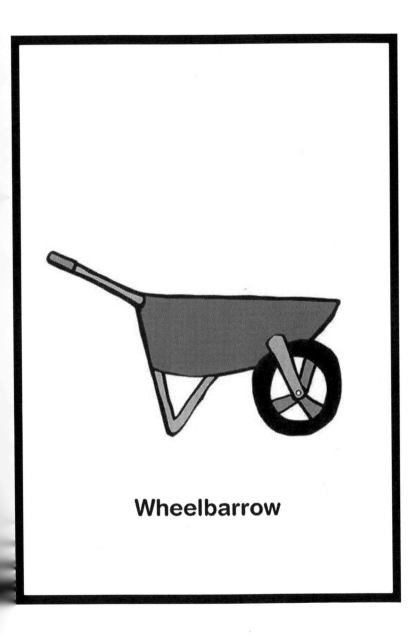

Wheelbarrow

Die Schubkarre

shoe-b-car-reh

Rake

Die Harke

hark-eh

Made in the USA
Lexington, KY
24 September 2017